# Color of my Breed

Fred Chavis

ISBN:9781793374189

# THE MT. OLYMPUS PLEDGE

I see Bear Jr. in every Pit Bull. Here is my pledge to them: I promise to love you unconditionally because this world won't. I promise to raise you in a consistent, responsible, and safe environment because this world won't. People will treat you differently. They will fear you because of the way you look. They will call you dangerous, violent, unpredictable, and a criminal dog. They will describe me the same way. As we go through this journey together, we will prove the stereotypes to be false and laughable. To me, you are a beautiful and amazing animal. Many dogs that look like you, are being mistreated and abused. We will put an end to this together. I pledge that when our work is done, you will be seen in the honor and glory you once adored.

# CONTENTS

# 1 REMEMBER THE PAST

"I'm living my best life, I said I'm living my best life, made a couple M's with my best friends, turned all my L's into lessons."

Rapping along to Cardi B and Chance the Rapper really helped me pass the time. I-95 in my opinion, is the worst highway to ever drive on. I thought to myself I should probably slow down--Cardi has a way of hyping me up. On 95, they have them helicopters tracking your speed. Everyone knows Virginia does not play. A black man in a Dodge Charger, one-time bruh!

"I'm like Big Pop, mixed with 2Pac. I'm like Makaveli," I continued my front seat concert.

I passed by one of those 'Authorized Vehicles only' signs.

Damn, there's a cop in the cut! Slow down, slow down, SLOW DOWN! Cardi talk lower! Let me get in the other lane, in between the other cars. I'll ride in silence, so he doesn't hear me. Man, here he comes. No lights yet. Keep going, please keep going. Go on one-time, go on! I ain't got time for this. I swear the police always bothering me. Man, dang! My mind was racing all over the place. I was panicking.

There go the lights, he saw me. Lord, please protect me--God, please. Today can't be my last day--not like this. Be respectful, Fred. Don't feed the stereotype. They think you're dangerous and uneducated --prove them wrong. Comply with his instructions.

As the officer walked to my passenger window, I rolled down my window all the way. I had nothing to hide.

"Do you know why I'm stopping you today?" the officer asked.

"No, I'm not sure sir," I answered.

"You were following that vehicle in front of you pretty closely and going a little fast," he said.

Well, why didn't you pull the car in front of me over? Why the hell did you pull over my black--oh, wait I just answered my own question. I was saying so much to myself. If I said these things to the officer, there was a high chance I may lose my life today. My heart was hammering on my chest.

"I wasn't following them intentionally and it's a good day, I just get a bit heavy footed on the gas," I said.

He then asked for my license and registration, which I already had ready in my hand. I was not going to be in a situation where I had to reach for anything. Officers always have their hands on their guns when speaking with black men.

"Where you heading Mr. Chavis?" he asked.

"My wife and I are heading to Maryland. She is driving ahead of me," I responded.

"What brings you all to Maryland?" he asked while glancing again at my license.

"My wife is going to be teaching in D.C. this upcoming school year and I am moving my company here to Maryland," I responded.

"What do you do for your company, Mr. Chavis?" he asked.

Dude, just arrest me. Stop giving me all this small talk. Do what you gon' do, I thought to myself. It felt every question was more of an interrogation than small talk.

"I train, advocate, and rehabilitate Pit Bulls," I answered.

"That's a great thing. I love Pits. They get a bad rep, but it's based on their environment. They deserve a second chance," he said.

"I tell you what Mr. Chavis. I'm going to let you go. Keep your speed down and good luck with the Pit Bulls," he said before handing me back my registration and shaking my hand.

Man, he is trying to play me. Pit Bull was probably a metaphor for Black. He's about to be like, sike, sike, dirt bike, you're going to jail, Mr. Chavis. Fred stop being negative, but I couldn't help but be negative.

What just happened? I was in complete shock. This was the first time; I had a positive interaction with a police officer. I prayed it would not be my last. I later would see that officer again at Chick-fil-a, while I told my wife what happened. He was just as nice as he was before and shook my hand again. Even with what is going on in our country, I know that there are still good, respectable cops out there. Unfortunately, we never know how to tell the difference and most of the time it is too late.

The officer and I shared a common belief that Pit Bulls are inherently good. It is indeed the environment and the owner that makes the dog. Likewise, for a person, the environment a person is nurtured in makes them the way that they are. Let me provide you with a bit of history on our beloved Pit Bulls.

For over 100 years, Pit Bulls were known as nanny dogs. They were known as great companions and protectors of their family. During that time, Pit Bulls were the most beloved dog in England and the United States. The Pit Bull heritage can be traced all the way back to the 1800s in the United Kingdom. Originally bred from old English bulldogs used for bull baiting. These dogs were put in a pit with bulls for hours, harassing the large bull until it finally collapsed from complete exhaustion. When bull baiting became outlawed, ratting took its place. This spectacle pitted dogs against rats to see which dog would kill the most rats in the least amount of time. The pit in Pit Bull comes from the pits the dogs were placed in for ratting. Old English bulldogs were not agile enough for the sport of ratting. The bulldog was crossed with terriers leading to our beloved Pit Bull Terrier.

In early America, Pit Bulls were your all-purpose dog. Their loving and loyal nature with humans, mainly children, earned them the title of nanny dogs and adored companions. Pit Bulls were a huge part of our culture. Mainly for the working class, who kept Pit Bulls close to the family. That is a very key point--remember that statement. One of my favorite movies growing up was the 90's version of 'The Little Rascals'. I aspired to be like my guy Alfalfa and I loved Petey. Petey the Pit Bull was my favorite dog ever--even beating out Chance from Homeward Bound. Petey was by far the most recognizable and loving dog of film history. He was a Pit Bull exemplifying the 'nanny dog' title. Petey was the child gang's most loyal and affectionate companion. He always provided the entertainment for his young pack members while also providing protection.

Ted Lucenay, Pete's owner, from the original series, once said, "Pete was a gentle, playful, and warm dog. He would sleep at the foot of my bed. He was just the regular family dog. I really miss him." Petey the Dog represented and lived up to the true demeanor of the Pit Bull, uncorrupted by humans.

During WWI and WWII, Pit Bulls were our nation's mascot. One of the most famous Pit Bulls was Sergeant Stubby. He was a Pit Bull that fought alongside our military during WWII. Sergeant Stubby displayed qualities of bravery, hard work, fearlessness, and friendliness. His bravery on the battlefield earned him much respect and honor.

How can a dog loved for generations, now be so hated? Take a moment to think about this question. This is your critical thinking assignment.

As many Pit Bull owners can attest, the nanny dog demeanor still lives in our Pit Bulls today. I remembered when I adopted my first Pit Bull from the local shelter. The first time I saw him was on the shelter's website. His eyes won me over instantly. The eyes of a Pit Bull say so much, with love and pain behind them. I knew I would adopt him at first sight. At the time his name was listed as 'Leroy' given by the shelter. When I adopted him, I changed his name to Bear Jr. When I first met Bear, it was instant love. Not for Bear though! That four-legged butthole completely ignored me. I was nonexistent to him. The day I went to go see Bear, I had visited with about 12 other Pit Bulls before finally arriving at his run. The shelter had so many Pit Bulls and I mean so many. If I could, I would have adopted them all. Visiting animal shelters is always a bittersweet experience for me. Even though I felt I saved a life, I still felt as though I left so many behind. So many Pit Bulls abandoned and longing to be loved again. Special shoutout to the selfless people that care for those dogs when selfish people abandon them.

When I entered Bear's run, he was a lot stalkier than his picture alluded to. I held out my palm to greet him. Man, I was so happy to meet Bear as he looked beyond my palm and stood in front of the gate opening. I could not believe the balls on him without actually having balls--the shelter had him neutered. I tried to call to him, but he still gave me nothing but his back, ass, and tail.

"Leroy! Come here boy!" I called.

The kennel attendant told me to try Patron. That was what his previous owners named him. I tried it.

"Patron, come here boi!" I called.

It worked! He turned and came to me briefly before going back to the gate opening. It was all I needed. I asked the attendant to get him ready, he was coming home with me.

My best friend wanted to be there when I adopted Bear, so I went back home, and then we arrived together to get my boy. Bear's adoption fee was $45. I couldn't believe the price for my future companion, but I do understand why the shelters do this. They are in a tough position when it comes to overcrowding, especially for Pit Bulls. If they can get more dogs adopted by lowering the fees or even waiving them, they will, in order to create space for more dogs. The cycle of dogs being surrendered to shelters never ends.

When we walked Bear out to the car, he jumped into the driver's seat with no hesitation. He was so happy to be free and able to drive again. We tried to explain to him that he didn't have a license, but he ignored our opposition. All we could do was laugh. I realized early on, Bear had quite the personality. Eventually, Bear did move to the back seat, and on the entire drive home I could not help but look at him. This beautiful Pit Bull in my back seat was heading home with me.

The week I brought Bear home, I was going through one of those college, roommate blood feuds. My roommate and I were not on speaking terms and he was avoiding me. I knew it was because to him, I was a so-called angry black man so I used this to my advantage. Now that I look back on it, I am ashamed for feeding into the stereotype. For those who may live under a rock, black people are often viewed as angry by their white counterparts--and, unfortunately, like most stereotypes, it has transcended to the group of people the stereotype was made about. In the black community we have become complacent with being labeled as the angry black person--being silent is just as bad as spreading the stereotype. Let me tell you, contrary to popular belief, black people are not angry-we are tired, agitated, and completely over our feelings being suppressed by not only the white community, but by our very own family members who tell us showing emotions are a sign of weakness and that we must always be aggressive and tough to reach greatness. Perhaps, there is some truth to us having to be aggressive. At the time, I could not help it. I wanted to drop kick his forehead. I considered this roommate to be one of my closest friends. A friend, where days were much better when we were on speaking terms. Our feud gave the apartment a gloom to it and put our other two roommates in an awkward position.

When Bear arrived, I allowed him to wander through the apartment to get familiar with his new home. Obviously, since ole dude and I were not speaking, I did not tell him I was adopting a dog, adopting a 40-pound Pit Bull. Bear being Bear, ran straight into his room. When I walked into his room to get Bear, he was knelt down petting Bear, while Bear was staring at me. Bear knew exactly what he was doing. An exchange of "what's up" led to a complete mending of our friendship. We had not shared words for months and Bear had mended our friendship in a matter of minutes. We are best friends even to this day.

Later in the week was more eventful. I left Bear alone in my room while I greeted some friends. Earlier in the day, I purchased my first pair of Jordans and a new pair of headphones--with my financial aid refund check. As I entered the room, Bear had my left Jordan shoe on the bed, mauled to death. I passed out. When I rolled over on the floor, there laid my new headphones--also chewed up. I couldn't believe this dog. My friends still laugh about that to this day. That was the last pair of Jordans I ever purchased. Bear taught me a valuable lesson that day.

Bear would go on to build further lasting relationships with the rest of my best friends, my crew, the brotherhood, the posse. He seemed to find a place in every heart he came in contact with. It did not matter who the person was, he remained the same sweet, loving boy to all. He had admirers from every neighborhood!

One of my roommates was actually scared of Bear. Bear was very aware of how he felt towards him and would abuse it daily. He would stare at him and then chase him into the kitchen. It was a fun game for Bear. Bear knew he was not allowed in the kitchen and my roommates were also aware, so the kitchen was the safe haven for scared, grown men to find refuge from big, bad Bear.

Bear was not a big fan of my other friend or maybe he just got a kick out of tripping him because he would trip him at least 6 times a day. That's 2,190 times a year. That was a lot of times to see my bald head friend eating the carpet while Bear just watched judgment-like. Bear made lasting memories and he was amazing with people.

He was just as amazing with other dogs. Any of my friends that had pets, no matter the breed or size, knew they had a playdate with Bear. When my boy, brought his Boxer, Dutchess, over I believe Bear fell in love. She was and still is a sweet girl to this day. They were snuggling buddies! Bear got into only one scuffle ever with a dog and this dog was owned by a then-girlfriend. I should have taken that as a sign to run the hell away!

I knew Bear was special the day I adopted him. He showed that many of the stereotypes attributed to Pit Bulls were indeed false. I made sure I nurtured this in him. He was my Petey. One thing Bear had in common with Petey, was his loving and gentle demeanor towards kids.

My wife came with baggage in the form of two sweet nieces, 'Lil Noodle' and 'Cooki Monsta'. Like what I did there with baggage, I know. My nieces loved Bear and he loved them back. They knew Bear would never hurt them, hence when they would chase him around, lay down on him, play with his tail, and the few times they got to walk him. The actual footage of this is absolutely cute. Bear remained gentle with them every moment. He was not a ticking bomb ready to explode as some individuals and groups would have you to believe. He was a teddy bear for his girls. Before Bear stepped in as the family dog for my wife and her family, Tiger owned that crown.

My wife grew up with a family Pit Bull named Tiger who passed away before meeting Bear at 16 years old. When I met him, he was a grumpy old man, but man did he live a beautiful, happy life. He lived a life fulfilled. They raised him from a baby to the old man I grew to love. They kept him close to the family and close to their hearts even until his last breath. At his passing, my brother-in-law buried him in the backyard so that even death could not do the family apart. Even now Tiger is still with the family. Everybody has their legends, and Tiger was the legend among Pit Bulls. I remember the day Tiger passed so vividly. I remember becoming emotional, thinking to myself about when the day would come that I too would have to say goodbye to my furry best friend. My heart, my life, my everything would be shattered. I held Bear very close that day.

Then that dreaded day came in January 2018, two months after me and my lady got married. Bear had passed away on my way home from complications with his meds. My heart and my life were shattered when I received the call. I remember speeding down Lake Wheeler Road in

Raleigh, NC at 80 mph. I was in complete distress. My legs felt like lead pipes as I stepped out of my car and made my way to what seemed like the longest run to the front door. My Bear was there on the floor, motionless. I could not believe it. Not like this God, I kept saying before I broke down hugging my sweet boy. There is not a day that goes by where I do not think about him. Bear and Tiger lived up to being nanny dogs. They fought the stereotypes that would have you to believe they are dangerous and not good family pets. How could someone even think they were not great pets for the family?

In 1976, the Animal Welfare Act was passed, making dogfighting illegal. Let's face it, illegal activity is attractive to some people. Once the act was passed, dogfighting began to reemerge with a vengeance. More people began to seek out Pit Bulls for the blood sport. Dogs that were once bred to love all and show friendliness towards strangers, were now being used as strictly guard dogs, protection dogs, status dogs, and fighting dogs. The demand for Pit Bulls began to rise with their increased use by the criminal element, especially dogfighting. Due to this increased demand, some individuals and groups saw this as an opportunity to become backyard breeders of Pit Bulls. They took into account no regard for temperament or socialization. They did not care to find a responsible home for the dogs to grow in. They were breeding Pit Bulls for the sole purpose of profit and violence.

This is where the nanny dog title began to diminish. Pit Bulls were now being represented in the negative persona of their owners' actions. Pit Bulls began to be associated with crime, thugs, and blackness. Even though dogfighting was and still is popular in the black community, black people were not the only ones involved in dogfighting. Dogfighters come in many different races and backgrounds, but black men were used as the face behind the sport.

Pit Bulls were being used for undesirable tasks, and a majority of their owners involved in other criminal activity. The Pit Bulls' reputation began reflecting that of its owners. Our Pit Bulls were caught in the middle of the Drug War and the rising popularity of dogfighting. At the height of the Drug War, black men were labeled as violent drug dealers. The media presented this narrative. The problem is that not every black man is violent or sells drugs, but that is what the media made America believe. The Pit Bull faced the same narrative, forcing the public to believe these dogs were dangerous. Pit Bulls became viewed only owned by those individuals involved in drugs and violence. The Pit Bulls' reputation was quickly diminished with all the stigmas surrounding them. Those stigmas Bear and Tiger surely did not deserve.

Since the 1980s, the Pit Bull has been vilified and portrayed as a monster and villain. The nanny dog repeatedly betrayed and outcasted because of irresponsible owners training them to be dangerous and aggressive. The change in how America feels and treats Pit Bulls represents a repulsive and underlying problem at the core of our country. A deep, deep issue of racial prejudice towards its black men reflected onto the Pit Bull.

# 2 DON'T FEED THE STEREOTYPE

Aggressive, violent, dangerous, untrustworthy, criminal, looks bad, suspicious, and uneducated are just a few of the stereotypes I have encountered. Stereotypes used to describe black men, like myself. Funny thing is Pit Bulls have also been judged similarly. Still, don't think the negative feelings towards Pit Bulls aren't a reflection of the racial prejudice towards its owners? I'll help you understand. Let's go back over 30 years.

In 1986, Congress passed the Anti-Drug Abuse Act during the height of the Drug War. The act made it mandatory for certain drug offenses to be punished with prison sentences. This led to a significant rise in incarcerations for non-violent drug crimes. This law, however, was racist in nature and intent, as it had one group in mind. Black men were being sentenced to prison for longer terms when caught having the same amount of crack as white Americans with cocaine. When Black Americans do drugs, its criminal. When white Americans do drugs, their sick and need help. People of color were being targeted, racially profiled, and arrested on only suspicions of drug use at substantially higher rates than whites. The results of the Anti-Drug Abuse Act led to disproportionate incarceration rates among people of color. If you were black and confronted by police, a jail cell was inevitable.

The following year after the Anti-Drug Abuse Act was passed, a Sports Illustrated story featured a cover illustration of a dog snarling, open-mouthed, with canines fully exposed. It was a menacing cover. The title read 'Beware of this Dog'. The dog featured was a Pit Bull. The media was similarly stigmatizing the black men during this time fully taking advantage of the public fear towards certain groups of people as it pertained to the war on drugs. A fear going back even to the production of Birth of a Nation in 1915. Black men were shown and treated as toxic carriers of drug addiction and social dysfunction. Comparing black men and dangerous animals or savage beast goes all the way back to the times of enslavement. Not much has changed even now. When discussing black men and Pit Bulls, social, economic, and legal context are purposely omitted from the analysis. Instead, we are portrayed to have some genetic or cultural flaw. We are portrayed to have some innate trait that causes us to do what we do-- inherently dangerous. Traits that justify why we are an inferior race to our white counterparts.

Erik Killmonger, sorry, Michael B. Jordan once said "Black males, we are America's, Pit Bull. We're labeled vicious, inhumane, and left to die in the street." He made this comment during an interview after filming for his upcoming movie, Fruitvale Station. For those unfamiliar with this movie, it was centered around Oakland resident, Oscar Grant. Oscar Grant was fatally shot by transit police, in manner witnesses described as execution-style. Fruitvale Station directed and written by Ryan Coogler, was a movie my heart could only take one time. This proved the point Michael B. Jordan was making. Black lives in America are expendable and don't matter. It explained why the Black Lives Matters's movement is met with so much opposition. This is a systemic problem in our nation. The police and justice system as a whole treat black men as animals, locking us up like animals, and murdering us like animals. We are America's Pit Bull and the Pit Bull is America's black men. This country was built on a foundation of hate, violence, and bigotry. It is no surprise that a country with a history full of prejudice towards groups and individuals because of their race, religion, sexual orientation, and other traits still has the problems of stereotyping and unequal treatment going on today. No, this country did not become racist only when Trump took office. It has always been racist, but the racists became bolder seeing one of their own as President of the United States. Just look at his Twitter feed.

The dictionary states, dehumanization is "the process of depriving a person or group of positive human qualities." The belief that black, brown, and other non-white people are lesser beings. The dictionary states "the consequences of systemic dehumanization of one racial group in a society can be horrific." This is evident today in the continuing incidents of police brutality consistently occurring in the United States. In 1991, when Rodney King was almost beaten to death in Los Angeles, the police officers who committed the act caught on video, said they were afraid. They did it out of fear for their lives. Multiple officers clubbing an unarmed, let me reiterate--an unarmed, black man and they were the ones in fear for their lives. This is a common defense of police officers to justify killing unarmed black men. Fear that leads to the killing of black women. Fear was used to justify the killings of Freddie Gray, Sam Dubose, Philando Castille, Terance Crutcher, Alton Sterling, Eric Garner, Oscar Grant, Jamar Clark, Jeremy McDole, William Chapmen II, Walter Scott, Eric Harris, Tamir Rice,

Sandra Bland (woman), Michael Brown, Antwon Rose Jr., Greg Gunn, Akai Gurley, Paul O'Neal, Akeil Denkins, Brendon Glenn, Botham Jean, Stephon Clark, Emantic Bradford Jr., Jemel Roberson, DeAndre Ballard, Robert White, Anthony Smith, Ramarley Graham, Manuel Loggins Jr, Wendell Allen, Kendrec McDade, Jonathan Ferrell, Jordan Baker, Victor White III, Dontre Hamilton, and so many others. Let's not forget Trayvon Martin who was racially profiled and murdered by the neighborhood watch's cowardly racist, who later exploited this tragic event for fame. He tried to register for celebrity boxing! What an absolute poor excuse for a human being. You murder an innocent 17-year-old black teenager and become a celebrity living your best life. You reap what you sow GeorgeyBoy. You better hope you never find yourself in prison--you will be the neighborhood bottom piece. Huge shout out to Jay-Z and his documentary series, Rest in Power: The Trayvon Martin Story.

The fear used to justify our murders are based on stereotypes, false stereotypes created from racist bigots. Stereotypes reinforced every day through the media and passed on from generation to generation. I consider the media the root of all evil. It would have you fear the victim and praise the murderer. Especially if the said murderer is white or wears the color of blue. The media twists around any story or event to persuade a gullible, bigoted nation that thrives on sensationalism. As in the case when different news outlets and 'The Donald' attacked Colin Kaepernick. Kaepernick kneeled because of all the unarmed, black victims murdered at the hands of our police force that resulted in no justice for the victims and their families. He kneeled for all the names and more that I listed earlier. He kneeled for change. The media would have you to believe he kneeled to protest the anthem, he kneeled to disrespect the flag, our military, and what our country stands for. You must open your eyes and see through the lies. Open your eyes and attempt to see beyond your own biased thoughts. Empathize with what Colin Kaepernick is actually protesting for. The media portrays him as the villain when in fact he is a hero. The  white power in our country fear different racial groups, different beliefs, different religions, and anything not 'American'. It will do anything in its power to defend it against such threats. It will do anything to keep America great. Patriotism and racism are a true love story.

People also fear Pit Bulls because of stereotypes--the false stereotypes reinforced through the media. This fear has led to severe consequences of alienation, brutal mistreatment, breed ban laws, and mass murder. Does this sound familiar?

Consider the publicity surrounding Trump's run for presidency and the turn of events once he was elected. Trump built a campaign based on fear. By invoking fear and hatred towards immigrants (Hispanics/Latinos, and refugees) Trump created a following of American people voting for him to save their white America from a hostile brown takeover. Too much? I'm not here to mince words. This country despises anything not American, not White. Trump's fear campaign led to all-out bans of Muslims entering the United States, travel bans still going on, and even the infamous wall to prevent Mexicans from entering our country. The media and Trump would have you to believe these actions were to protect the United States and its citizens, but that is not true. They have exploited fear through media sensationalism to persuade the American people that Muslims, immigrants and Hispanics/Latinos are here to hurt us, that they are very dangerous people.

Think back to recent events where a mass shooting has taken place and the shooter responsible was said to be Muslim or an illegal immigrant. This individual was deemed a terrorist and the heat was once again put on banning these kinds of people from entering America. Think about the stories surrounding unarmed black men being gunned down by police. The victims are portrayed as gangsters having violent ties to crime and drugs in the hopes to justify the police officer's motive to remove them from this world. Now, I want you to think about recent events, where a mass shooter was white, such as the white supremacist that killed nine African-Americans in their own church. They present these individuals as suffering from a mental illness. They begin to fight for more resources to be directed toward helping these individuals suffering from such an infliction. White male murderers are portrayed as loving family men or having suffered from traumatic events that justify their actions. The turn of events is completely, unsurprisingly shocking. I am so sick and tired, tired and sick of the lies and false narratives. Call it what it is, acts of terrorism. White males who are the danger to society proven by statistics, not stereotypes. When a white man decides to kill, many people usually die. When a white man, a racist white man, decides to end lives of those different from him, they are not feared by police. They are operating in the hidden agenda of this country. They are taken into gentle custody and provided with food and warmth. However, many argue that black men like myself are more dangerous. Do you see where I am going with this? Why is a white man who murdered 9 people not deserving of death by your standards, but a black man running from police is?

Media sensationalism, according to Oxford, is defined as "the use of exciting or shocking stories at the expense of accuracy in order to provoke public interest and excitement." This means the stories the media presents, purposely neglect certain truths to sway public judgment towards the desired outcome, such as creating fear and hate towards an individual or group. Most people who have strong hatred and bias towards Pit Bulls have never owned one or even been in close proximity to one. How can someone have such strong, negative feelings toward something they have never experienced being around? This is what media sensationalism accomplishes. When a labrador retriever fatally harms a child, it remains local news. Switch labrador retriever to Pit Bull and it becomes national headlines. Labradors do not invoke fear in people. Pit Bulls do because they have been portrayed as the villain. In fact, if a labrador were to hurt a child, all information from the event is examined. The labrador's reputation remains untainted as it is defended to the magnitude of it being a dog and some human error had to have taken place. The story almost always stating the dog had never shown aggression before and were an absolute loving family member.

Pit Bulls do not receive the same support. Instead, their breed is bashed and verbally slandered throughout the story. They are portrayed to have been prone to aggression and that no human error took place. The Pit Bull is not presented as loving, family dogs. The media will say the breed was prone to violence and aggression and that the dog lived a life in and out of shelters. This story will then move to promote the solution in the form of breed ban legislation.

Unarmed black men killed by police are not presented as family men or great dads. They are shown as a danger to society, their criminal background, if any exists, is displayed for the world to see in order to slander and smear them as a human being undeserving of life. The media acts to justify the police officer's reasoning to murder this individual.

The media capitalizes on the fear of the public. It promotes false narratives and false stereotypes. The truth is, any dog, that has been mistreated and abused can be dangerous. The individuals that feed into the stereotypes and innate aggression of Pit Bulls display a core misunderstanding of the true nature of not just Pit Bulls, but of all dogs. I despise statements that feed into the stereotypes of Pit Bulls. Statements like "you should own Pit Bulls at your own risk", "always be on the defensive", "stay one step ahead of your Pit Bull to prevent their aggression", and "Pit Bulls are ticking time bombs." My personal favorite, "Pit Bulls are naturally aggressive so they must be socialized early." All dogs, not just Pit Bulls should be socialized. Any dog that is not properly socialized, can develop negative reactions to certain stimuli. This is the owner's responsibility to raise them in a responsible home. Pit Bulls, just like any other dog, have individual personalities that are shaped and molded through the environment in which they are raised. They are inherently good unless you raise them to be different. No dog is naturally aggressive. If they are raised to be friendly toward other dogs, they will be. Don't feed the stereotype!

Another popular stereotype spread about Pit Bulls is that they have locking jaws. When they bite down, you can't get them to release. A naturally aggressive dog with locking jaws; talk about fear. One politician even said Pit Bulls have the bite force equivalent to that of a shark. Bro, go home and grab a Snickers. That's crazy talk! Statements like this, feed the stereotype and help give the Pit Bull its' undeserving, bad reputation. Pit Bulls do not have the bite force of a shark or a hippo. A dog's bite force is directly correlated with the size of their body and skull. Dogs with larger heads tend to have a higher bite force. This is proven science. Larger heads usually mean larger jaws. German Shepherds, Rottweilers, Mastiffs, and numerous other breeds have higher bite force than Pit Bulls. Don't feed the stereotype!

Do not let anyone tell you Pit Bulls are not good family dogs. They weren't known as nanny dogs for over a century for no reason. Nothing has changed in our Pit Bulls except the narrative. Any responsible owner of a Pit Bull can attest their desire to be part of and close to the family. Their true nature is playful and loving towards the family, especially children. Don't feed the stereotype!

When I was growing up in Boston, Massachusetts--Dorchester to be exact--I was made to believe the previously mentioned stereotypes. I feared Pit Bulls when I was young and not just Pit Bulls, but all large dogs. Any dog that displayed aggression towards me, I feared and associated it with being Pit Bull. What scared me the most as a child was hearing, "you can't trust a Pit Bull," and "that they turn on their owners." I could go to Franklin Park Zoo--where my dad worked--every day and look at lions, condors, panthers, gorillas, bears, and snakes with no fear, but I was afraid of dogs. Afraid of Pit Bulls. I guess it was because there were no stereotypes surrounding the zoo animals.

It wasn't until I got a little older and my family would take the train to go visit my mom's best friend, Ms. J, in Natick, Massachusetts that I got over my fear of dogs. She was a responsible, caring person who loved dogs and cats. She had a very loving and gentle nature about her and it reflected in her dogs. When I first met her dogs a German Shepherd and a lab mix named Chief, I was so mortified I embarrassed my dad and cried. He smacked me on the back of the head like Bernie Mac used to do annoying Jordan on the Bernie Mac Show. Okay, no he didn't actually do that, but I'm sure he wanted to just like the first time he took me swimming and the first time we drove through a wild safari--I cried both times. That all is beside the point though. Ms. J was very gentle and patient with introducing us. She would have me reward them with treats and pet them when I felt comfortable. Before the day was over, I loved those dogs. Chief and I created a terrorizing friendship. I realized her dogs were not like the dogs I saw in my neighborhood. They weren't raised the same. When I was much older, I realized the difference was the environment in which the dog grew up in. It was how the owner raised their dog. Not only did Ms. J show me what dogs can be like if raised in a responsible and loving environment, but she introduced me to the Harry Potter books written by the amazing JK Rowling. Absolutely, one of the best things that have ever happened to me! Thank you, Ms. J,!

Pit Bulls do not turn on their owners. The top quality of Pit Bulls is their unwavering loyalty. Why would a dog so loyal turn on their owner? Their loyalty, besides courage, is why many owners, especially those with bad intentions, choose to have Pit Bulls. Their drive to please their owners, no matter the deed trained to do, is unquenchable. Don't feed the stereotype!

What I saw growing up and still see today is Pit Bulls being used as guard dogs, tied out in their owner's yards. Pit Bulls are great protectors of their family, but they are not guard dogs. Do you understand that statement? Do you understand the difference? Pit Bulls are great protectors of their family, but they are not guard dogs. Let me explain. Pit Bulls have a friendly nature and are naturally friendly and accepting towards strangers. Ignore the stereotypes. They are great at assessing different situations and determining if a situation is threatening or non-threatening. It is an innate ability. If the situation were to arise, God forbid, a Pit Bull will defend its family with its own life. They love their family unconditionally and more than they love their own self. They do not have to be trained to do this. Remember they want nothing more than to be close to their family. When you see Pit Bulls tied up outside, isolated from their family and barking at every approaching stranger, this is unnatural. Isolating your Pit Bull in this manner is neglectful, abusive, and creates an unbalanced, unpredictable dog. You the owner are responsible for how your dog turns out. I can't tell you how many times a stranger was approaching and Bear didn't even react or acknowledge them because it was non-threatening to me. If he did react, best believe he was wagging his tail for attention. Guard dogs are not accepting to strangers and in some cases will attack a stranger if they encroach on the territory, they have been tasked with protecting. This is not the Pit Bull way. Pit Bulls you see in the yard displaying aggressive behaviors have been neglected the love they most desire from their family. It angers me to see Pit Bulls neglected in such a way. I had a client that owned a young Pit Bull puppy named Rocky, who spent two weeks with me for 14-day training camp. His owners wanted him to be a guard dog, meaning he would be outside most of his life, alone. Rocky was a very sweet pup, soon to be transformed into the stereotypes I fight against. I must have told his owners 80 times to not pursue this route. It was like talking to a wall. The hardest thing I've had to do since beginning my company was to finally tell these people I would no longer be offering my services to them. I never heard from them again and there isn't a day that goes by that I don't wonder about Rocky's wellbeing.

One thing that helps me come to terms with Rocky's case, is seeing my other Pit Bull clients doing so well and raising their dogs with love. One of my favorite clients was a Pit Bull as beautiful as her name, Lily. When I first met Lily and her owner, they didn't flinch at the sight of me. Lily's owner was very welcoming and kind--Lily mimicked this and welcomed my presence. Lily and I built a strong bond. She was always down for me. The day after Bear passed, I continued to take care of my clients. I would always record all my sessions on my GoPro, but on that day, I shut it off. While I was out with Lily, I broke down crying over Bear. I remember kneeling on one knee on the sidewalk and Lily came up to me and put her head on my shoulder. I just held her for a few moments until I got myself back together. Lily, like most Pit Bulls are very sensitive to their owner's emotional state. She was an exceptional Pit Bull and the last Pit Bull that Bear got to hang out with. Her owner proved that it is how you raise your dog. Most dogs resemble their owners, not in appearance, but in their personality. Pit Bulls need more owners like Lily's and less owners feeding the stereotype.

Pit Bulls are not inherently dangerous. Stop feeding into the stereotypes that portray black men as dangerous to justify our killings. We are not dangerous people. The greatest said it best, "I ain't-a killer but don't push me." Pit Bulls are inherently good and loving despite what the media would have you to believe. The fear of certain dogs is a direct reflection of the fear of certain people. Fear that has led to police brutality and breed specific legislation. This fear and prejudice have led to innocent pets being taken from their homes and murdered.

# 3 THE B.S. LAW

Let me tell you a story about Ginger and Whiskey. No, I'm not talking about a really good drink. I am talking about two beautiful, sibling Pit Bulls. Ginger is a white and brown Pit Bull. She has a brown patch over her left eye and a special brown patch at the top of her tailbone that resembles the ginger root, hence her name. Whiskey is all brown with white paws and a white patch on his giant chest. These two puppies are inseparable from each other and especially from their new family's six-year-old twin boys. Their new family rescued Ginger and Whiskey from an abusive owner when they were only 8 months. The previous owner would beat them and withhold food in preparation of their life as menacing dog fighters. He was caught when a friend of his, stupidly, went on Facebook Live while he was trying to force the siblings to attack and kill a restrained rabbit. He was yelling at them and repeatedly striking them throughout the hard to watch video. Anybody who owns Pit Bulls, are very aware of their super-sensitive demeanor. This was evident when I would play Madden and yell at the TV when a 330-pound defensive tackle would run a 4.3, 40-yard dash and chase down my created quarterback; Bear would run out of the room. I would always say "I'm fine" and he would return. What Ginger and Whiskey endured in this video and their early short life was heartbreaking. Ginger and Whiskey did not know what it was like to be loved until the Lawrence family rescued them.

When the pups first came home with the Lawrence family, they were very timid and would run at the sight of food. You could tell they were starving but were scared to eat--scared to trust the hands providing the meal. The pups were only familiar with being repeatedly beaten soon after the food was placed down or the food was removed before they could have a second bite. The family remained very patient. Each member of the family would place handfuls of food on the floor of the room the dogs were in. The children especially enjoyed doing this because they were able to take on big boy responsibilities. To help with the anxiety the pups felt, they would leave the food out and leave the room. They loved these dogs and would do everything they could do to earn the trust and love of the two beautiful dogs. Eventually, the pups realized the food was not going to be removed and no more beatings.

Ginger was a strong female; she led the siblings out to eat the food. Soon they were eating out of their new family's hands. The pups fell in love with the twin boys immediately. They created so many memories together, napping with the kids, chasing the kids, and licking food from the kids' messy faces. Ginger and Whiskey were truly loved by their family and they loved them back. The pups had their own little doggie room to sleep in and go to for peace and quiet, but of course, they wanted to sleep closer to the family. They would drag their beds to the kids' room to sleep with them. Funny thing is, they always ended up in the bed with the boys. Their parents thought the boys were moving their beds into the room with them until they caught the dogs in the act--frozen like a deer caught in the headlights.

Birthday parties, holidays, football Sundays, Ginger and Whiskey were full participants. They were there through thick and thin--whether it was a sneaky, huge bite out of the birthday cake, stealing the Thanksgiving turkey, barking at the scary pumpkin man on the porch, and even crying with Mr. Lawrence when he continuously lost in fantasy football. This was more Whiskey as Ginger showed no interest in fantasy football. The funniest moment was the video where Mrs. Lawrence told her two Pit Bull children that they weren't actually humans. They were dogs. The look of sadness and betrayal on their faces was undeniable.

A few weeks later, the neighborhood association held a doggie day event for the opening of the new neighborhood dog park. Their neighborhood had quite the population of dogs and this was a great gesture by the association. The Lawrence family planned to attend with what they called the 'cul-de-sac gang'. Ginger and Whiskey enjoyed many doggie play dates and would definitely enjoy the event! There was, however, one neighbor in the cul-de-sac, the Lawrence family did not get along with-- their old neighbor, Ms. Tess, and her just as old and obese miniature poodle, Abigail. Abigail was super aggressive and had attacked many neighbors, delivery people, and lawn care providers. Ms. Tess would always insist it wasn't her fault or Abigail's fault. Instead, it was the victim's fault, because Abigail was very sweet. She just got nervous around 'certain' people. Ms. Tess was not thrilled when the Lawrence family moved into the neighborhood. She was even more upset when she realized they had rescued not one, but two Pit Bulls. She despised Pit Bulls, not from her own personal experience, but based on what she heard and saw about them.

She would make it a point to appear in traumatized fear at the sight of them. The only thing she feared more than Ginger and Whiskey, was Mr. Lawrence. Evident when she called the police on him while he was coming back from his routine morning jog. She told the police and other neighbors she did not recognize him and he looked suspicious. She, of course, issued no apology for the horrible incident, that ended with Mr. Lawrence in handcuffs outside of his home. To add insult to injury, she also called the cops on the Lawrence family's twin boys for being too loud while playing in the cul-de-sac. Mrs. Lawrence went off on that old racist, lady. She made it clear she better not ever put her kids' lives in danger again. Needless to say, the Lawrence family had a history with Ms. Tess and nothing would change how they felt about her.

The 'cul-de-sac gang' agreed they would meet at the Lawrence house and walk over together. First to arrive was the McCloud family and their American bulldog, Honey. Honey got along great with Ginger and Whiskey, as good as the drink. The McClouds had no children, only Honey. When she arrived, the tripod was complete!

As they all headed out, the other neighbors gathered at the driveway. It was a beautiful day for doggie day. Everyone was hyped and excited and the dogs were feeding off of all the energy. Duke was there with his German Shepherd, Kevin. He had Kevin, trained by a military dog trainer. He never put that dog on a leash, but for the most part, Kevin remained by his side until he was given the command to go play and be normal. The Knight family had also walked over. They had 2 gorgeous little girls and two Great Danes named Hades and Zeus. They were a very sweet family that always wore Crocs. All you could hear were the crocs clicking the ground as they were dragged over by Hades and Zeus. As the kids began to run around each other, the group began their walk to the new dog park. Mr. Lawrence made it a point to walk Ginger and Whiskey on the left side of the street where Ms. Tess' house was. She was checking her mailbox when she saw the group approaching. She picked up a barking Abigail and tried to perform what looked like a sprint up her hilly driveway. It was the most dramatic scene, everyone just walked on by purposely ignoring her. Hades and Zeus were pulling the Knights ahead--the crocs probably made it hard to keep step. Mr. McCloud was walking Honey alongside Mr. Lawrence, Ginger and Whiskey as they would jump on each other every few moments to remind each other of their presence. The kids were all running around in circles around Duke and Kevin, trying to entice Kevin to chase them. Kevin remained by Duke's side almost like a drill sergeant and his combatant.

The gang was getting close. You could hear the dogs barking and having fun in the dog park. The entire neighborhood association was there, including the president of the association, Jessica. She was super annoying, super nosey, and super entitled. She had a lab named Chloe that caused quite the uproar in the neighborhood among the male dogs as she was not spayed. Jessica refused to have her spayed because she did not want to take away her womanness. She rarely spoke to anyone in the group. For some reason this time, she was walking right towards them. She greeted Duke before addressing the group. Without looking at the Lawrence family, she informed the group, that their dogs, weren't allowed in the park or the event. She then pointed at Whiskey and Ginger before drawing her attention to Honey.

"That dog is not allowed either," she said.

The group was in complete shock. The kids were curious about the conversation between the grown folk. The dogs were becoming anxious.

Jessica continued, "These dogs are dangerous and have been banned in the neighborhood. This was voted on and unanimously agreed on. Many of the wonderful people living here have felt threatened by their presence. I assume you may be unaware, but our county just approved the Pit Bull ban, effective immediately. I would get rid of those beasts as soon as possible."

She then turned around and walked away. Duke issued his condolences as he followed Jessica into the dog park. The Lawrence family, Knights, and McClouds all stood in disbelief at the news they had just received. There was a lot to sink in as the dogs had now become agitated at the lack of movement and the restraint from entering the dog park to socialize. The Knight family decided they would not attend the event since their good friends could not. Instead, they would all head back to the Lawrence home. As they walked back not only did they have to explain to their kids what had just occurred, but they also had to console their dogs who seemed just as disappointed as the kids. On their walk home, Whiskey's bandana fell to the ground almost symbolizing the events of today. Ms. Tess was back on her porch as the families walked past seeming satisfied with the interaction that had just transpired. Seeing the smug look on her face made walking by her home just that more irritating.

When they all arrived at the house, the kids and dogs immediately ran out into the massive, fenced in backyard. They had already forgotten the previous ordeal, but the adults had not. As the dogs and children played, Mr. Knight kept an eye on them while Mr. Lawrence was getting the grill ready. The outdoor beer fridge was already loaded and the nice day was lightening up the vibe. The lingering issue that was still bothering the families, was what was the underlying reason for the breed ban? Meanwhile, the dogs and children were racing through the yard while Honey, Ginger, and Whiskey zigzagged between them. The most spectacular aspect of the view was how fast the Knight girls could run in their crocs. Hades and Zeus were lying next to the gazebo staying in the shade.

"What exactly does this breed ban mean?" asked Mrs. Lawrence.

"I wouldn't listen to anything Jessica says. She lives to enforce her power on us minorities," said Mr. McCloud.

"I don't know man. I can't stand her either, but if what she says is true our dogs are no longer safe here," responded Mr. Lawrence.

"How would they enforce that?" asked Mrs. Knight.

"I'm sure that if Ms. Tess learns of the ban, she'll make sure it's enforced here, however they do it," said Mrs. Lawrence.

"Let's just take it day by day. Maybe this whole thing will just blow over," said Mr. Lawrence as he was heading out to the yard alongside Mr. Knight handing him a much-needed cold beer.

The dogs were now running through the yard with Crocs in their mouths as the children gave chase. It was a happy moment that carried a gloom to it.

Over the next few weeks, the Lawrence family no longer took Ginger and Whiskey out for their usual long walks. Instead, they just let them out in the privacy of their backyard. They even canceled Ginger and Whiskey's upcoming vet appointments. Nothing saddened the family more than to deprive their beloved dogs of essential walks and vet care. Their safety was the utmost priority right now. They wanted to avoid any and all trouble. The county breed ban was indeed a horrific reality. It had already become known through the news and social media that Pit Bulls and similar dogs were being put down, some were taken from their homes before meeting their end. It was the purge, except this one was not going away after 12 hours. Pit bulls and their families were being targeted. Their beloved dogs being murdered. Some owners were facing jail sentences, even after their pets were confiscated. The Lawrence family were in a horrible predicament and they knew it.

One afternoon, the family arrived home to find a notice on their front door. The notice was from their county animal control. It stated they must surrender over Ginger and Whiskey. Failure to surrender their Pit Bulls would result in the dogs being forcibly removed from the property with a $1,000 fine and/or up to 6 months in prison. This was the day they dreaded. They knew for their children's sake they could not risk jail time. Mr. Lawrence had contacted his parents immediately after hearing the news. They agreed to watch the dogs until they could figure out a more permanent solution. It was currently Tuesday and they stayed 3 hours away. The family would take a road trip there on Friday after the kids got out of school.

On Friday morning, the family headed out to take their kids to school. The McClouds were also heading out. Honey was out in the yard giving her goodbye. When they arrived at the school, the boys promised they would be on their best behavior, and Mr. and Mrs. Lawrence would bring Ginger and Whiskey to pick them up.

When the Lawrences arrived back home after dropping the boys off, Honey was still out in the yard chasing the breeze and anything else that moved. Today was one of the few days the couple were home together with no kids. It was time for grown people things. They changed into their pajamas, lit incense, and pulled back the covers. They went straight to sleep for about four hours. It felt great to just sleep. When they finally got up, they turned up. While making omelets and mimosas for brunch, they jammed out to some Jaheim. Ginger and Whiskey looked on side by side, judging them for every missed note during the awful karaoke session.

That's when the doorbell rang followed by that undeniable knock on the door. Mr. Lawrence opened the door to two animal control officers and one police officer. Another cop pulling up to the house before Mr. Lawrence could even ask "how may I help you, officers?" It was already clear why they were there. They had come to take Ginger and Whiskey. Mrs. Lawrence was in the back room holding both dogs close to her as Mr. Lawrence spoke with the officers. Ginger began to whine sensing something wasn't right, Whiskey following her behavior.

There was no negotiating with the officers. No extending deadlines or trust in good faith they would surrender the dogs at a later time. They were not leaving without Ginger and Whiskey and they proceeded to enter the house.

Mr. Lawrence looked back at his wife with tears down his cheek. He was angry, sad and helpless. They were helpless. This would be the last time he saw his dogs, his other two children. Mrs. Lawrence began to sob uncontrollably as Ginger stood behind her. She turned and fell to her knees as she hugged Ginger tightly. The animal control officers were closing in on Whiskey who was standing in front of the ladies. His rigid posture told how he was feeling. He was not going to let these intruders hurt his family. This was a threat to his pack. The police officer took the strap off his holster and put his hand on his gun. Mr. Lawrence swiftly got between them, while having his hands high in the air. He grabbed Whiskey by the collar, knelt down in front of the large Pit Bull, and placed his hands around Whiskey's large head. As he looked into his dog's yellowish, green eyes, he kissed his forehead before saying "I love you baby boy." The animal control officer placed the noose cable from the restraining pole around Whiskeys neck and then they forcibly began to drag him from Mr. Lawrence's arms and their home as he shrieked and whined. His tail tucked completely under him.

Ginger was next and Mrs. Lawrence was not letting go of her girl. Mr. Lawrence stumbled over to his wife as they group hugged Ginger who was whining and shaking. "We love you so much sweet baby girl," they said repeatedly and the noose cable now went over Ginger's head and around her neck. They began to drag her away. Her screams broke the family down even more. She began to urinate as she was dragged from her home. The Lawrences managed to gather the strength to follow them outside as Ginger was being dragged away. Whiskey was in the truck barking frantically. Ginger was able to look back at her owners one last time before she was loaded onto the truck with Whiskey. Mr. Lawrence could not do anything but hold his wife tightly as she cried into his chest. How would they live without them? What was going to happen to their furry babies? Do Ginger and Whiskey blame them for this? Most of all, how would they tell the boys?

Honey had come back out into the yard after hearing all the commotion. The officers turning their attention to her as they began to make their way into the yard. Honey began to bark and growl before taking a lunge at the officer. Mr. Lawrence yelled "No" at the top of his lungs to no avail. A gunshot followed and another immediately after.

"Don't look", Mr. Lawrence said to his wife as he held her back close to his chest.

You're probably asking yourself was this a true story. The truth is, what happened to the Lawrence and McCloud family is a reality for many dog owners in areas where Pit Bulls are banned through BSL. Breed-Specific Legislation (BSL) or the B.S. Law as I call it. It is a law that fully bans or sets restrictions for certain types of dogs based on their appearance. The appearance of a perceived dangerous dog breed, such as Pit Bulls. BSL may present itself as either a ban or laws of restriction an owner must adhere to if they own a dog on the ban list. A breed ban requires that all dogs of a certain appearance of breed be removed from the area where the law is enforced. Think about what happened to the Lawrence family. These targeted dogs are then subject to be killed by animal control. If a targeted breed, such as Pit Bulls are allowed to stay in a ban area, the owner is usually held to a strict set of breed-specific restrictions, such as wearing a muzzle in public, displaying a 'vicious dog' sign outside their property, and even purchasing liability insurance. Breed specific legislation are absolutely monstrous laws. Dogs with no history of aggression or behavior issues are destroyed because of their appearance, because of their breed. Each and every dog, just like every person is an individual and should be treated as such. Yes, a dog is a dog and they do not think in the same sense a human does, but each dog exhibits their own unique personality.

Pit Bulls have only known life as victims. If you own a Pit Bull look into your dog's eyes. A Pit Bulls' eyes are full of much pain and sorrow. Their eyes are the windows to their amazing large hearts full of so much love to give. Take a trip to your local shelter in your city. Especially, those shelters located in the inner-cities. Due to their undeserved stigma, a ride to the shelter is almost always a one-way trip for these dogs. In most cases, a death sentence. In the United States, Pit Bulls are the most abused, abandoned, and euthanized breed. They have been brutally and inhumanely killed by angry neighbors and aggressive police. In Mesa, Arizona, a man burglarized his neighbor's home and shot their Pit Bull twice in the head while the dog was secured in its crate. The man said in his statement it was completely worth it. In inner cities, Pit Bull owners know their dogs will not survive encounters with police. Police are infamous for killing Pit Bulls when entering these homes. This is why I appreciate so much about what that Virginia trooper said to me. These dogs rarely receive a second chance at life--the shelters overflowing with Pit Bulls. Adopt don't shop.

To vilify, ban, and murder these dogs is a despicable and hateful act. The individuals who set these ordinances and commit such acts, display an extreme level of ignorance and prejudice. This ignorance of dogs and prejudice towards the Pit Bull has led to shameful actions with murderous intent. The breed-specific laws surrounding Pit Bulls are more vicious than their supposed reputation.

Take Prince George County in Maryland for example. Prince George is a predominantly black county. When Washington D.C. began to gentrify its communities, many black families moved to the lesser cost of living in Prince George County. Breed specific legislation is in full effect there in the form of a breed ban. PG County prohibits owning, keeping, or harboring of a Pit Bull Terrier within the county. According to their law, Pit Bull Terriers refer to the Staffordshire Bull Terrier, American Staffordshire Terrier, American Pit Bull Terrier, and any dogs that have the appearance of being predominantly made up of those breeds. Predominantly means that the dogs exhibit the physical characteristics of a Pit Bull more than any other dog breed.

Back in 2015, The Best Friends Animal Society estimated there were roughly 178,000 dogs in Prince George County, about 13,000 being Pit Bull terrier-like dogs. Based on the numbers of Pit Bull terrier-like dogs, the non-profit animal welfare group estimated it cost the county between $250,000 to $500,000 each year to confiscate, maintain and dispose of Pit Bulls in their county. This is a very steep price to maintain an ineffective ban. The officials responsible in PG County hoped this ban would be effective at eradicating all the Pit Bulls from their community but they failed in that objective. Groups like the Maryland Dog Foundation continue to push for repeal of Prince George County's archaic law.

Breed specific legislation is ineffective at its objective, costly to maintain, and overall does not enhance the public's safety. Instead, it persecutes families with innocent dogs and fails to capture the reckless owners that have created dangerous dogs through abusive and irresponsible methods. The B.S. Law focuses on the breed and appearance rather than the dog and human interactions. The laws divert resources such as animal control and law enforcement and then uses those resources to deal with non-threatening family dogs.

One of the biggest issues with BSL is the difficulty in identifying Pit Bull-like dogs. According to Pitbullinfo.org, 50% of Pit bull type dogs are misidentified. Fifty, effin percent! Yet, 100% of the cities that have active BSL occurring continue to see serious bite-related incidents. Maybe because when it comes to dog bites, it's not a breed-specific issue. In 2017, there were at least 12 different breeds involved in fatal dog attacks further proving this is not a breed-specific issue.

When a fatal dog bite occurs, if the dog has any bit of terrier or resemblance of terrier, it is mislabeled as a Pit Bull. So, for those that like to play the numbers game and state Pit Bulls contribute to the majority of fatal dog bites, you are mistaken and your numbers do lie. In fact, you can compare these claims to my personal favorite statement, 'He fit the description'. Breed misidentification plays a significant role in the stigma attached to Pit Bulls. Pit Bull owners are often faced with being the target of social prejudice, physical and verbal attacks, and BSL.

You do not have to be a unique owner to raise a Pit Bull because of their supposedly dangerous reputation. You have to be a unique individual to deal with the daily b.s. that comes along with owning one--I'm sure many Pit Bull owners can attest. If you're a white Pit Bull owner, you get to experience for the first time in your life a small taste of what it is like to be hated, stereotyped and systematically oppressed. If you are a black Pit Bull owner, well, life just got a lot harder for you. All Pit Bull owners go through a lot for their dogs, but as a black owner, I must emphasize our experience is much different, much worse.

After I adopted Bear, one of the biggest obstacles we faced was finding a place to live that allowed Pit Bulls. I was still in college, so a house was out of the question. I was broke as a joke! All the college apartments obviously did not allow Pit Bulls. I went on several of these glorious apartment tours close to North Carolina State University (Go Pack!) only to find out after I had fallen in love with the place that they had breed restrictions. Pit Bulls were not allowed, no exceptions. Five places straight, same story. I preferred to visit potential apartment homes rather than call. I hated talking on the phone, still do! I got to the point that before I even gave my name, I would ask if they allowed Pit Bulls. When they said no, I turned right back around for the door. This was the same story for many Pit Bull owners.

One leasing consultant, after informing me they did not allow Pit Bulls, still asked if I wanted to tour their community. Why the hell would I do that? I would never get rid of Bear even if I was allowed to live here for free. That entitled idiot then told me that they were offering two free months of rent on a 12-month lease. He told me he was sure the money I would be saving was more than how much it cost me to buy a dog. Wow. First, drink a gallon of gasoline, light a match, swallow it--and I didn't buy, I adopted!

Not only do Pit Bull owners have to deal with breed specific legislation where they live, but if they are trying to find a home, you have to deal with apartment pet policies that may not allow your dog to stay there and neighborhood associations that also do not allow your beloved dog to live there. Some owners, like myself, have to pass on many places because we refuse to get rid of our dog. Other owners, having different circumstances, may have to come to terms with the fact they may have to surrender their Pit Bull for their home. A sad truth.

After providing a temperament letter and an outrageous pet deposit, my wife and I were able to secure a townhome in upper Raleigh for us and Bear. Our new home was a corner unit with a dog park located right behind us in a large, open field. There were a lot of dog families there all making use of the dog park. There were only 4 Pit Bull homes, including our own; Lucky, King, and Sam. Sam was owned by a white lady and was the only one of our group welcomed to the dog park for their evening neighborhood playtime. The rest of us never joined in for the fun times. It was in this neighborhood, I began my dog training business, Mt. Olympus Animal Services. When my wife and I would take Bear out for our peaceful evening walks, it was almost immediate that the people in the dog park would freeze and stare--wondering if we were going into the dog park, which we weren't.

Don't worry, you all are safe. We are taking our blackness and dangerous dog on a long walk.

We would usually bump into Lucky and his family on these walks. Lucky was a 100-pound puppy that literally adored the ground Bear's paws walked on. He was a regular client of mine. After we all talked for a bit, my family would continue our trek through the larger neighborhood where the big houses and the golf course were. It was this portion of the walk where we would be treated as dangerous beings. Some people would literally cross the street to avoid us. Some people would walk by us without even the slightest greeting or eye contact. Most days security would drive back and forth by us. One day security actually stopped us, and let's just say my beautiful, black queen let him know real quick, that ain't gonna fly here!

Of course, people were treating us this way because we had a Pit Bull, but there was another factor as well--our blackness. People were afraid and treated us as beneath them because of how we looked, because of the color of our skin. When it was just Bear and I on walks, I should have just worn a prison jumpsuit and put a chewed-up cat in Bear's mouth. That was the way our white populated neighborhood treated us.

This one lady would even let her dog poop in our yard next to our cars in the driveway and would not pick it up. Are you kidding? Nothing pushes me like a neighbor allowing their dog to defecate on your land without even the slightest regard or respect to pick up after their pet. The dog park was literally 20 more steps from our property. It took us some time to figure out the culprit, but when we did my wife confronted her one morning while she was actually in our yard again. Let's just say the shit stopped. Man, I have an amazing woman. I knew if I confronted the lady, there was a high probability that the police would be called on me for being portrayed as an angry black man that threatened her.

Many of our neighbors allowed their dogs to run throughout the neighborhood off leash. A privilege a Pit Bull owner would never have. My next-door neighbor exploited this daily. Some days and weeks, I would have Pit Bulls that I was training at my home. The last thing I wanted was to step out of my garage with Tyson and an off-leash dog runs up on us. I asked over and over for them to stop the practice by my home, being polite each time until I finally had enough of their entitled, crap. One day, I walked Tyson and Bear out together. Tyson was a large Pit Bull with a huge head, a head too big for his body. At this point, Tyson had completed his training and was not excited or distracted by the loose dogs. I told my neighbor; I was going to let my dogs off leash as well. You know, since, you disregard me every day. Let's have a nice little playtime. I knew my dogs would not hurt my neighbor's dog, but I also knew my neighbors were slaves to the stereotypes of not just Pit Bulls but of me. They began to put the leashes on their dogs with a quickness.

Why have your dog off leash out here, when the dog park is literally right there? Not to mention, your dog has growled at us on numerous occasions. I've been nice and asked you all over and over to stop allowing your dogs off leash around my home. I'm done being nice. Next time, I will call Animal Control on you and I have video proof. If I let my dogs off leash, you all would be afraid and call the cops. Get over yourself. Not everyone appreciates and respects your entitlement. Have a great day entitled pricks.

After this, my wife and I knew we had to go. The people in the neighborhood were bad for business and bad for my sanity.

One thing is true for all Pit Bull owners, no matter the race, we want our Pit Bulls to experience life to its fullest like any other dog. There is not one animal welfare organization that supports BSL. The United States Center for Disease Control (CDC) decided to also not support BSL. The CDC cited the inaccuracy of dog bite data and the difficulty that comes with identifying dog breeds accurately. They stated, "as certain breeds are regulated, those who abuse and exploit dogs by making them aggressive, will just find a new breed to use," for their unjust cause.

Through the breed neutral county laws already in place, there is no offense an owner can commit that is not covered. This includes, but is not limited to, nuisance laws, running at large laws, dangerous dog laws, pet limit laws, leash laws, and cruelty and neglect laws. BSL is not the answer. We must ban and punish the real beast.

# 4 BAN THE BEAST

Karen Delise, author of Fatal Dog Attacks: The Stories Behind the Statistics and The Pit Bull Placebo: The Media, Myths, and Politics of Canine Aggression has over 20 years of research and investigation. She is Research Director for the National Canine Research Council and is considered our nation's leading expert on dog bite-related fatalities. She has been very influential in shifting public perspective towards canine aggression by redirecting focus on reducing the risk through proper humane care, custody, and control of companion dogs. Karen Delise stated:

> My study of dog bite-related fatalities occurring over the past 5 decades has identified the poor ownership/management practices involved in the overwhelming majority of these incidents: owners obtaining dogs, maintaining them as resident dogs outside of regular, positive human interaction, often for negative functions such as guarding/protection, fighting, intimidation/status); owners failing to humanely contain, control, and maintain their dogs (chained dogs, loose roaming dogs, cases of abuse/neglect); owners failing to knowledgeably supervise interaction between children and dogs; and owners failing to spay or neuter dogs not used for competition, show, or in a responsible breeding program.

Thank you, Karen, for your insight and research.

Human failings have led to a bad reputation for Pit Bulls. Pit Bulls just like any other breed become what you train them to be. Due to their undeserving stigma, Pit Bulls are the choice dog for the criminal world and irresponsible owners. Pit Bulls just seem to attract the worst kind of owners. Why is that? They are perceived as dangerous dogs that are fiercely loyal. The fiercely loyal part being 100% accurate. No matter how terrible they are treated, they strive to please their owners. They remain loyal to the worst kind of people. These are the individuals that should be held accountable. These people are the real beast.

The criminal element has victimized the best qualities of the Pit Bull. If you think these owners are using clickers and treat pouches to train their dogs, you are in for a major plot twist. They aren't using any kind of positive reinforcement. Instead, these beautiful, loving, big hearts, on four stubby legs, are being beaten, starved, chained, tortured, and murdered. They are being trained to kill and if they don't kill, they are punished. If they don't eventually get with the program, they are killed in horrific fashion as to make an example out of them. It is a vicious cycle. These individuals are the real beast.

Dogfighters are major, MAJOR, contributors to the suffering of Pit Bulls. Dogfighting is one of the most monstrous, evil, and heinous forms of animal cruelty. Dogfighters are a very diverse group of people ranging from many ethnicities, locations, and backgrounds. This is a very important fact because the media would have you associate dogfighting and Pit Bull violence with only blackness and people of color. There are an estimated 40, 000 members in organized dogfighting rings and even more street fighters. Even though dogfighting is illegal and a felony in all 50 states and in Washington D.C., the blood sport still occurs. The fact that Pit Bulls are the dog of choice in dogfighting, is what many use to justify breed specific legislation.

The life of a dog involved in dogfighting is a life that brings me to absolute tears. I am a huge empathizer and when I hear stories of dogfighting, I put myself in that situation. I put my own beloved pets who I care deeply about in that life of pain and suffering. It's a tough thing to imagine, I know, but I ask that you do the same as you continue to read my book.

Fighting dogs are forced to live their lives in complete isolation and restrained by heavy chains. In city areas, most of the dogs may not ever see the light of day being kept in basements and other secluded areas. The fights often take place in basements, garages, abandoned buildings, barns, outdoor fighting pits, warehouses, and even the streets.

The training methods these dogs endure are nothing short of extreme violence and torture. To start with, fighters will modify their dogs' appearance by cropping their ears and docking tails through the use of inhumane methods. This is a look many breeders fashion their dogs to look like. This is something I will never understand. These modifications limit areas another dog can latch onto during a fight and reduce any hints or cues given off from the dog's normal body language.

When it comes to training dogs for dogfighting it always involves the torture and killing of other animals. The other animals are considered bait animals and are utilized to test a dog's fighting instinct. Bait animals always end up dead in the process by the intended dog, another dog, or the murderous human. What is terrifying about 'bait animals' is that they are mostly stolen pets, puppies, kittens, small dogs, passive Pit Bulls, animals from shelters, and animals obtained from sources like Craigslist. I want you to look at your dog or pet right at this moment. I want you to think about something, you don't want to imagine. I want you to imagine yourself in the shoes of one of the owners that have endured such a loss. Can you imagine your beloved pet being taking from the comfort of your loving home? Your pet being lured into a stranger's vehicle, drooling for the reward of the yummy treat these sick individuals presented to snatch up your pet. On the ride to their dogfighting operation, your dog is sitting in the back seat. At first happy, because you raised them well and they love people, only these people that have your dog are soulless fucking individuals with no fucking heartbeat. Your beloved pet begins to feel anxiety and worry. They begin to feel something isn't right. The occupants in the car are laughing and verbally abusing your dog because your dog is scared and just wants to go home. Your dog misses you and begins to bark and whimper.

You know what the passengers do? They hit your dog repeatedly before duct taping their mouth completely shut. When they arrive at their home or place of cruelty, one of the passengers carries your squirming dog into the home. When they enter the home, your dog becomes increasingly frightened. The place smells like dogs in pain, it smells like dead animals and blood. They then throw the dog into a pit located in the basement. The one window in the basement is painted black, the lighting is very dim. Your dog sits in this room for hours alone before hearing approaching footsteps, loud voices, and paws now coming down the basement stairs, closer and closer. The footsteps stop at the entrance into the pit and there are multiple large dogs, waiting outside the pit growling ferociously, and barking. The gate then opens, and the dogs are released into the pit.

If you are a pet owner and animal lover, that was excruciatingly hard to read, I know. Imagine how families that have had to endure that feel. I would hate for such an end to come to one of my beloved pets or clients. Imagine how it feels for the dog trained and forced to kill. Dogfighters are not just animal abusers; they are killers with no remorse and a danger to society. If you think the only crime, they have a part in is dogfighting, you're mistaken. The individuals and groups who fight dogs usually do so as a part of other criminal enterprises such as drugs, firearms, racketeering, trafficking, and violent crimes. No matter their race or background, they are a danger to society. You have to be a sinister being to participate and spectate the monstrosity. No one wins in dogfighting from the perspective of the dog. Both animals, if they survive the battle, suffer major puncture wounds, lacerations, broken bones, and serious blood loss. The losing dog being thrown away or left like garbage, killed, or brutally tortured and executed by its owner in order for them to regain some ounce of their manhood back. God says to love your enemies. I'm not there yet. If you're a dogfighter and you just happen to be reading my book; your day of reckoning is coming. I have dedicated my life to end you and your abuse. Your day of reckoning is coming.

Irresponsible backyard breeders supply and contribute to dogfighting and have overbred the breed. Shelters are overflowing with the Pit Bulls they breed. Their motive is strictly for profit. They take no regard of providing a responsible home. No regard for socialization. No regard in ensuring that the dogs they breed find a happy, permanent home. These individuals are literally destroying our amazing breed and sending thousands to their death. If you are the kind of breeder, I described this is for you. Go visit some local shelters and see the dogs that you contributed to being there. If you have any bit of human in you, it should break your heart to see all the Pit Bulls in shelters, many on death row. Stop contributing to the over breeding of Pit Bulls. Cut off your supply to known criminals and invest in your dogs by finding responsible homes. Make a difference in the war against our Pit Bulls by investing in the well being of your dogs!

As Karen Delise confirmed through her extensive research--poor ownership and management practices were the major contributor to fatal dog bites. I cannot say it enough, human failings have led to the Pit Bulls bad reputation. Irresponsible owners are to blame. Many owners raise their dogs in ways that reinforce the negative stereotypes surrounding Pit Bulls either through ignorance or purposeful intent. Pit Bulls make great family dogs and should be kept close to the family. Some owners think Pit Bulls make great guard dogs and leave them outside all day and night to patrol, isolated from the family and much needed human interaction. The dogs are allowed to free roam or are restrained by chains and tie-outs. These Pit Bulls become imbalanced and some develop territorial aggression. This is not natural and these owners are making their Pit Bulls into something they were not intended to be. Please know, any breed of dog in this situation would have the same results. True Pit Bull owners know these dogs are 100% house dogs and want to always be around you. They want nothing more than to be loved by their family --so please fulfill and nurture their needs. Do not make them into something they are not. You are only feeding into the stereotypes and contributing to their bad reputation due to your irresponsible ownership. To isolate them like this is abuse and neglect. If this is your intended use, please do not own a Pit Bull.

Irresponsible owners fail to provide a responsible environment for their dogs, but they also fail in providing a consistent home. Lack of socialization, rules, and boundaries contribute to the opposing sides war on Pit Bulls. Socialization to other dogs and humans is essential in not just Pit Bulls, but all dogs. If you do not have time for a dog, simply don't get one--

it's not fair to them. They look to you in the way they should behave and treat other dogs and people. If you fail in this aspect, you also fail that innocent dog. A majority of the Pit Bulls described and judged by the media are those owned by these irresponsible owners that fail to socialize and train them consistently.

The unfortunate situations that arise because of this are solely on the owner, not the dog. There are some Pit Bull owners that have endured truly, tragic events, where the dog attacked a loved one such as a child. I want you to know, you not only have my empathy, but I sympathize to your plight. There are a tiny number of attacks, that simply can't be explained. It is a rare event, that a well-raised, family pet with no prior past of behavioral issues hurt a human. One thing that cannot be forgotten or overlooked is that a dog is a dog and a dog is an animal. This is very important because many of these unfortunate incidents could have been prevented with responsible ownership. No matter how long your dog has been in the family, it is always good to supervise your children with dogs.

When Bear was still with us, we would always take family trips to my mother-in-law's house. My wife's brother would always be there with his beautiful family, that included his two daughters, my nieces. I knew Bear would not hurt them, but I still was sure to always supervise their time together. As a dog owner, you must be able to recognize the signs that your dog may be becoming agitated or may need a timeout from the situation. When I would notice Bear becoming tired from all the attention and playtime, I would let the girls know so that Bear could go take a much-needed nap. Dogs do not speak; they cannot tell us they need a break or to stop. They either try to avoid the situation or guess what they may bite or nip. To be a responsible dog owner you must be able to recognize the cues given by your dog's body language. Unfortunately, in some of these tragic incidents, the parent and dog owner, failed to recognize or acknowledge the signs. They failed to provide proper supervision. This may sound harsh, but it is not the dog's fault. It is not the breed's fault. It is on the owner.

Nowadays, many parents do not take any responsibility for how their kids turn out. They blame it on other elements but never blame it on their lack of parenting. You see this in many high schools where parents are allowed to attribute their child's misbehavior and lack of effort to their 504. Some of the students absolutely qualify for this, but some are abusing the system, making excuses to not be parents. Parents use the 504 as their scapegoat to avoid responsibility. When it comes to incidents involving Pit Bulls, the Pit Bulls make the perfect scapegoat. It is so easy to blame the breed based on their negative reputation than to take responsibility for your hand in the event.

Human failings have led to unfortunate situations involving Pit Bulls and their undeserved bad rep. Irresponsible owners that do not train, interact with or socialize their dogs are to blame. Individuals that raise their dogs to fight and those that contribute to over-breeding of the Pit Bull are to blame. They make the job easy for biased government officials to impose breed discriminatory laws. They make the job easy to purge out our Pit Bulls.

# 5 EQUITY

My goal is not to bring further divide among the different races. Trump has already done that. My goal is not to bring division among the different groups that advocate for Pit Bulls tirelessly each day. I support every last one of those groups. I am providing the black perspective. I am bringing to light the issues a black, Pit Bull owner faces. I am bringing to light the motive behind Pit Bull prejudice that has more to do with the type of owner associated with them than the breed. I not only fight for our Pit Bulls, but I fight for Black Americans in this country that face social injustice every day.

This country consistently dismisses the struggles, fear, and racial prejudice that my people go through every day. There are no days off. This country dismisses the black experience as some fairytale that exists in our minds. This country refuses to acknowledge and empathize with our plight. I guess that's the point of privilege, you don't have to empathize with those you consider to be beneath you. Until this country and its' inhabitants acknowledge racial prejudice towards black people and until this country stops portraying black men as a threat--Pit Bulls will continue to face the same storyline because BSL and other prejudice are not about them. It's about the black men that own them.

I am angry when I hear stories of animal abuse towards Pit Bulls. I need to emphasize this point--I am angrier when I hear about another unarmed black man murdered by the police. Many put animal life over humans when the loss of life is black. Just recently, an Arkansas deputy was fired after shooting a dog for barking at him. When an officer has shot an unarmed black man, the officer is placed on paid or unpaid leave--even if there is video footage to prove their guilt. Many people fight for Pit Bulls and fight against animal abuse with the ferocity of Spartacus, but are numb to the racism black people in this country have to endure every day.

As a black man, my fight does not end with Pit Bulls. I fight for equity in the black community. If this country continues to see the black man as a threat, they will continue to see our Pit Bulls as a threat. We are indeed connected whether you want to acknowledge it or not. Taking photos of Pit Bulls with smiling white Americans, in order to present them as less threatening does nothing, but reinforce the notion that black men like myself are dangerous. It does nothing, but strengthen the false assumption that by taking Pit Bulls from the hands of a black man and into the hands of a white individual, it saves the breed. I call this the Superhero Effect. The Superhero Effect, is when a white person with the means to make a difference through wealth and other resources chooses to help and improve a certain condition such as low-income communities. The people mean well, they want to help, but they go about it the wrong way. They end up hurting the people they intended to save. Trying to re-label the Pit Bull as something different than Pit Bulls in order to save them from the stigma does not save them. Saying we are not going to call a Pit Bull a Pit Bull because of their reputation is to me like saying "I don't see color" when I tell you I'm experiencing racism. The Pit Bull name is not the problem, just like the color of my skin should not be a problem. People that say they don't see color mean well, but they do not realize they negate the experiences someone like me experiences. They negate the fact that the way I experience life is different from them. The problem I have with this--is diversity should be celebrated. Our differences should be acknowledged and accepted. We are people from many different backgrounds and races-- that is what makes life beautiful. I want people to acknowledge the fact that I am a black man and accept me for who I am and not what people stereotype me to be. The Pit Bull should be celebrated for being a Pit Bull. You cannot run from the stigma--you have to face it.

Black men are not dangerous simply because we are black. We are not dangerous simply because of our appearance. Pit Bulls are not dangerous simply because of their breed and appearance. I want equity for my black people.

Breed specific legislation is racially motivated. Take another look at Prince George County in Maryland It is a predominantly black county and BSL has been enforced for more than 20 years with advocates unsuccessful in their efforts to have it overturned. The ban arriving around the same time more black people began to call PG County home after being forced to leave D.C. due to gentrification. These black families bringing their Pit Bulls with them.

If you can acknowledge the prejudice Black Americans face, you can better defend Pit Bulls. The government officials that set the laws must be forced to come face to face with the racial intent of their laws. The prejudice surrounding Pit Bulls is more about the perceived type of owner than the dog. To win this fight, we must stop feeding into the stereotypes against black men and our community. I desire to see more representation from the black community joining in this fight--more black men proving the stereotypes false. We are not a threat, but we must not feed into the stereotypes that America has for us. Our community has helped contribute to the bad stigma of Pit Bulls. We must change this and defend our dogs.

Remember the past. Pit Bulls deserve a chance to go back to their days of glory and honor--absent of abuse and discrimination. Stop feeding the false stereotypes that would have you see the Pit Bull and its' owners as a danger to society. Instead, fight against racially motivated laws that seek to punish our Pit Bulls because of the prejudice towards its owner. We must ban the true beast from owning and hurting our dogs. We must hold those individuals accountable and make sure they cannot continue to operate and hurt more of our Pit Bulls. Hold the irresponsible owners responsible for the actions of the dogs they raise. Most of all, we must fight for equity, not only for Pit Bulls but for minorities. We are at war against racism.